Diversity

of

Life

The Five Kingdoms

Lynn Margulis

ENSLOW PUBLISHERS, INC.

Bloy St. & Ramsey Ave.	P.O. Box 38
Box 777	Aldershot
Hillside, N.J. 07205	Hants GU12 6BP
U.S.A.	U.K.

Library of Congress Cataloging-in-Publication Data

Margulis, Lynn, 1938–
      Diversity of life: the five kingdoms / Lynn Margulis.
          p.   cm.
      Includes bibliographical references and index.
      Summary: Describes how scientists classify living organisms into
groups known as kingdoms, and the characteristics of each.
      ISBN 0-89490-278-4
      1. Biology—Classification—Juvenile literature. [1. Biology—
Classification.]
QH83.M363   1992
574'.012—dc20   91-44773
                                                                                CIP
                                                                                 AC

Printed in the United States of America

10 9 8 7 6 5 4 3 2 1

Illustration Credits:
Barbara Dorritie, p. 52; Christie Lyons, pp. 6, 21, 26, 32, 40 (top), 43,
47, 58, 61; Cornell University, p. 23 (left); Emily Hoffman, p. 42; Ilyse
Atema, p. 28; J. Steven Alexander, pp. 30, 31, 49, 56, 67; Kathryn
Delisle, pp. 11, 14, 50, 51; Kenneth Estep, p. 41; Laszlo Meszoly, p. 37;
Sheila Manion-Artz, pp. 18, 40 (bottom); William Ormerod, p. 63.

Cover Illustration: © Peter J. Bryant \ Biological Photo Service

Contents

Acknowledgments

We wish to thank all those who helped us produce this little book. Dorion Sagan wrote the original Sciencewriters first draft, which Ilyana Klein reorganized. Thomas Lang and Mark Friesen provided valuable assistance with manuscript preparation, as did René Fester, Polly Cherau, and Lorraine Olendzenski. Stephanie Hiebert contributed so much to the book that she could be considered a co-author.

This book supplements the five kingdoms teacher's guide and poster classroom activities described on page 77. We thank Louise Armstrong (Ethyl Walker School), George Nassis, and Kenneth Rainis for development of explanations of five kinds of life ideas for students and teachers. The Richard Lounsbery Foundation, New York City, provided financial assistance that helped make this work possible.

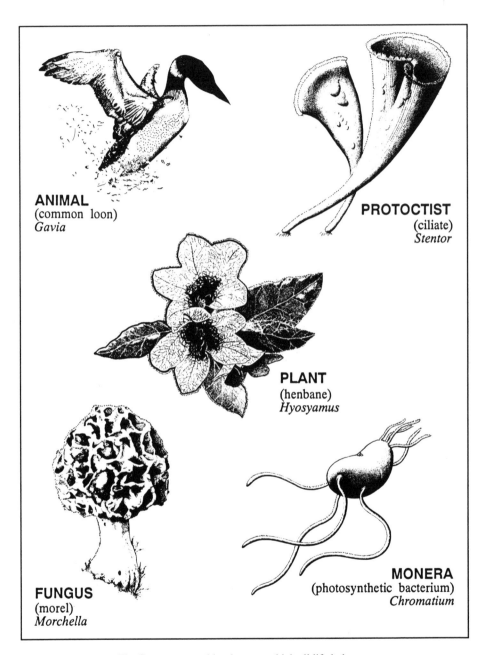

ANIMAL
(common loon)
Gavia

PROTOCTIST
(ciliate)
Stentor

PLANT
(henbane)
Hyosyamus

FUNGUS
(morel)
Morchella

MONERA
(photosynthetic bacterium)
Chromatium

The five groups or kingdoms to which all life belongs.

1

Introduction

This book is about life on Earth and how living organisms are classified into groups. Deciding what kinds of living things exist—in other words, how many groups there are—is trickier than it seems. Scientists observe live organisms carefully. They try to group living things together based on similarities such as the shape of their bodies and how they move and reproduce.

For a long time people thought that all solid things (objects that take up space and have weight) fit easily into one of three categories: animal, vegetable (plant), or mineral. Any living thing was either an animal (because it moved) or a plant (because it was green and needed sunlight to make its own food). If neither animal nor plant, then it was not alive at all and therefore was called a mineral.

Now, most scientists agree that there are five kinds—or kingdoms—of living things on Earth today. Some scientists believe that there are only three kingdoms of life, but everybody believes that the old two-kingdom system, which classified all living beings as either plant or animal, is no longer the best.

In this book we discuss the five-kingdom classification system, which consists of the following groups: Kingdom Monera (bacteria—microbes that have no nuclei in their cells), Kingdom Protoctista (seaweeds, amebas, and other strange living beings that have nuclei in their cells), Kingdom Fungi (molds, yeasts, and mushrooms), Kingdom Animalia (animals), and Kingdom Plantae (plants). Although it is certainly not perfect, the five-kingdom system recognizes that a world of life exists whose inhabitants are decidedly neither animal nor plant.

You might have heard about a "revolution" in biology. We all know from newspapers and magazines, movies and videos, that the biological sciences have changed vastly in recent years. Genes from certain animals have been isolated in test tubes, and totally new proteins have been made outside of living bodies. To understand the current biological revolution, we must first understand organisms that are neither animals nor plants.

Most live beings that are not animals or plants belong to large groups of organisms that some people have never even heard of because they are not obvious parts of our everyday experience. If they are neither animal nor plant, what can they be? Where do they live? How do they live? How should they be classified? Into what groups should they be placed? How are they related to animals and plants? What role do they have in the revolution in biology today? This book answers these and many other questions about the great variety of life on Earth.

2

History of Classification

The process of making up categories like "animal" and "vegetable" and deciding which things go into which category takes up a lot of time in science—and in thinking in general. The science of dividing and arranging things—including identifying and classifying organisms—is called taxonomy (which comes from the Greek word *taxis,* meaning "arrangement").

Taxonomy is very important to biologists who classify all living things, including organisms as different from each other as beetles, rose bushes, and human beings. People have been watching living beings and trying to classify them into groups for a long time. The names and classification ideas have changed through time as more has become known about the process of living and the kinds of life on Earth.

Aristotle

The Greek philosopher Aristotle (384–322 B.C.) was probably one of the first to try to classify living things. A student of Plato (427–347 B.C.), Aristotle founded his own school, the Lyceum, where he taught his students as they followed him around. Aristotle was more modern in his thinking than many scholars who followed him. For example, Aristotle classified dolphins with land creatures rather than with fish. He did this because dolphins bear live young and nourish them before birth through a special system of blood vessels and connecting tissue called a placenta; the placenta connects the unborn infant to its mother's womb, the special organ where the fetus grows. Even though the shape of a dolphin makes it look more like a fish than a mammal, Aristotle saw that dolphins share many characteristics with mammals.

A keen observer of nature, Aristotle classified over 500 animal species. Although sometimes he was completely wrong (for example, he believed that boys came from hot sperm and girls from cooled sperm), in many cases, such as that of the dolphin, he was right. Still, his correct view that dolphins are more like land mammals than fish was overlooked by later writers for almost 2,000 years.

Pliny

During the time of the Roman Empire, the scholar Pliny (A.D. 23–79) wrote his *Natural History,* a 37-volume work that drew upon over 2,000 even more ancient books. The work focused mainly on zoology (the study of animals). Pliny described many kinds of animals, including unicorns, mermaids, flying horses, and monstrous men who used their giant feet as umbrellas to shade themselves from the sun. Based more on rumor and fable than on actual observation, Pliny's *Natural History* does not relate much to scientific fact, but it does represent an excellent attempt to organize and catalog all available information about life on Earth.

The Middle Ages

During the Middle Ages (about A.D. 500–1400), after the fall of the Roman Empire and before the rise of modern science, many fantastic creatures were rumored to exist. Medieval scholars wrote books called "bestiaries" that described imaginary beings (Figure 1) similar to those that many people today believe exist, such as Big Foot, the Loch Ness Monster, and the Yeti (or Abominable Snow Man). Most of these made-up animals were said to inhabit far-off regions, making it easier for people who had never seen them to believe in them.

The discovery of fossils and skeletons of unfamiliar life forms also helped kindle the belief in mythical beasts. Someone who has never seen an elephant before and then finds an elephant skull might imagine that it belonged to a giant man, just as dinosaur bones were once thought to be ancient birds. In fact, the Chinese once believed that the fossil teeth of sharks came from dragons. (To this day shark teeth are sometimes called "dragon teeth".)

John Ray

In 1686 the Englishman John Ray (1627–1705) published a catalog of plant life, containing 18,600 different species of plants, that was far more scientific than Pliny's collection of animal species. In 1693 he also

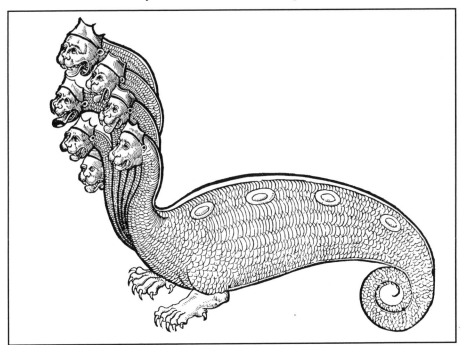

Fig. 1: A sixteenth-century woodcut of a many-headed hydra, from a book of ancient woodcuts. Scholars wrote books describing beings like this.

classified animals in a logical manner, arranging them by similarities and differences in their hoofs, toes, and teeth. (Aristotle had used similar clues when he wrote that no animal had both tusks and horns.)

With new writings by Ray and others, the medieval stories of fantastic creatures were taken less seriously. A careful observer and thinker, Ray dispelled some of the mystery when he wrote in 1691 that fossils came from plants and animals that no longer lived on Earth. The study of nature was gradually becoming more scientific; no longer did it depend merely on gossip or what others had written or illustrated in ancient books.

Linnaeus

Our modern system of classifying organisms began with the Swedish scientist Karl von Linné (1707–1778), more commonly known by the Latin version of his name, Carolus Linnaeus. He revolutionized the naming and identifying of living beings. In his system, called binomial nomenclature (binomial means "two names"), every known type of organism has two names, a genus and a species name.

The genus name always comes first and begins with an upper-case letter, but it functions like the last or family name of a person because it assigns the organism to a larger group. The genus name of the ostrich is *Struthiocamelus,* whereas that of the cassowary (another large bird) is *Emeu* (Figure 2). Other genera (plural of genus) you might know include: *Rosa* (roses), *Pinus* (pine trees), *Gorilla* (gorillas), and *Rhesus* (a kind of monkey).

The species name functions like a person's first name by identifying a specific organism within the larger group (the genus). The species name always follows the genus name and begins with a lower-case letter. For example, *Homo sapiens* refers to human beings. *Homo* is our genus name, and *sapiens* is our species name. (In Latin, *Homo* means human, and *sapiens* means wise.) *Canis familiaris, Canis latrans,* and *Canis lupus* are the scientific names of the domesticated dog, the coyote, and the wolf, respectively (Figure 3). The

Fig. 2: A drawing of two flightless birds, the ostrich from Africa (above) and the cassowary from Australia (below), by a naturalist in 1678.

genus name *Canis* groups these three similar animals together, whereas the species names—*familiaris, latrans,* and *lupus*—identify each animal as a separate, unique organism within the larger group.

In scientific writing the technical name of an organism (that is, its genus and species names) is always italicized or underlined. No matter where in the world scientists work, they all use the same genus and species names to refer to a particular organism. International scientific terminology is an important benefit of taxonomy. Even scientists who normally write with Japanese or Russian letters use the Latin alphabet to identify organisms. They can work together and understand each other, even if an organism has different common names in different places.

For example, some people call the same flowers either daffodils or jonquils; other people call only certain kinds of daffodils jonquils.

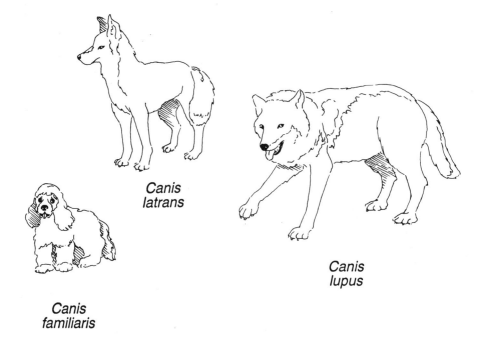

Canis latrans

Canis lupus

Canis familiaris

Fig. 3: The wolf and all domestic dogs are very closely related to each other and to coyotes.

When these groups of people get together to talk about flowers, things can get very confusing. Fortunately, each different flower has its own unique scientific name. Using scientific names, these people can be sure that they are referring to the same (or to different) flowers.

In addition to developing the system of binomial nomenclature for the genus and species of each organism, Linnaeus also arranged organisms into larger categories. As Charles Darwin (see page 19) put it, he "grouped his groups." Linnaeus arranged genera together into orders, and orders together into classes. Later, Georges Cuvier (1796–1832) arranged orders into phyla. Followers of Linnaeus expanded this scheme and continue to do so today.

Linnaeus inspired nature lovers to depend on observation to name and categorize all life on Earth. Species is the smallest category; species fit in genera, genera fit in families, and so on. The table on page 16 uses the human being as an example to show how Linnaeus' classification system works. Human beings are classified within the species *sapiens* in the genus *Homo*. Extinct ancestors of humans— along with all people—are in the family Hominoidea. All hominoids (members of the family Hominoidea)—along with apes, monkeys, lemurs, and other similar animals—are in the Primate order. All primates—along with cows, bats, whales, and other animals with fur—are in the class Mammalia. All mammals—along with other organisms that have backbones, including birds, fish, reptiles, and amphibians—are in the Vertebrata subphylum, and so on. In this way, smaller groups are included in larger groups from species all the way to kingdom. We belong simultaneously to all the groups listed in the table.

Linnaeus believed that each of the different species was created simultaneously by God. Yet by noticing close relationships among organisms, Linnaeus helped prepare the way for the discovery that all species are related by common ancestors and therefore must have evolved through time.

Classification of People

Taxon	Example	Characteristics	Some Other Members
KINGDOM	Animalia	blastular embryos	cockroaches jellyfish
PHYLUM	Chordata	hollow nervous system, gill slits	sea squirts sharks
SUBPHYLUM	Vertebrata	backbones	bony fish birds
CLASS	Mammalia	hair, mammary glands	rats, bats
ORDER	Primates	teeth, and other skeletal characteristics	monkeys apes
FAMILY	Hominoidea	upright posture	*Australopithecus* (fossil apemen)
GENUS	*Homo*	tool making and using	*Homo erectus* *Homo habilis* (fossil people)
SPECIES	*sapiens*	culture and language	all people today

Linnaeus' classification system was appreciated so much that a crater on the moon was named after him. As new information has become available, Linnaeus' system has changed in many ways, but today we still use his naming system for many species, genera, families, and other groups.

The Influence of the Microscope

Understanding life forms that are neither animal nor plant, most of which are far smaller than we are, requires that we enter their world. With microscopes we can see, like Alice in Wonderland did, that there is another world that exists parallel to our own. Right now, right here, we are coexisting with a densely inhabited world containing all sorts of strange, tiny creatures. To be able to describe and classify the inhabitants of this other world, which is always with us even if we ignore it, first we must see it. The opportunity to view this subvisible world arose for the first time in the seventeenth century.

After the first lenses were manufactured in Holland in the 1600s, the Italian astronomer Galileo (1564–1642) invented a tube with a magnifying power of 32 (that is, it enlarged an image 32 times). He used this first telescope to look at the skies and the craters of the moon. When the tube was turned around, it served as a microscope. A Dutchman, Anton van Leeuwenhoek (1632–1723), was the first person to put the microscope to good use.

Carefully grinding his own lenses to make single-lensed microscopes that could be used with light from an oil lamp, Leeuwenhoek made the best microscopes of the time (Figure 4). A cloth merchant, he needed magnifying lenses to inspect his wares, but as he delved deeper into the microscopic world, he soon found cloth, however beautiful, to be boring.

He began looking at hair, skin, muscle, and blood cells; he examined slivers of ivory and scrapings from teeth. He looked at excrement and his own wriggling sperm cells. He studied peppercorns, expecting to find sharp barbs that would explain why they tasted so spicy, but observed cells instead.

To his astonishment, Leeuwenhoek often saw tiny, fast-moving creatures. He described them as little animals, or "animalcules." As long as they could swim or were not green, the little beings seen by Leeuwenhoek and his successors were classified as *protozoa*, which means "first animals." Today we know that the term protozoa should be avoided because these single-celled organisms are not animals at all. A better word for these single-celled organisms, including the

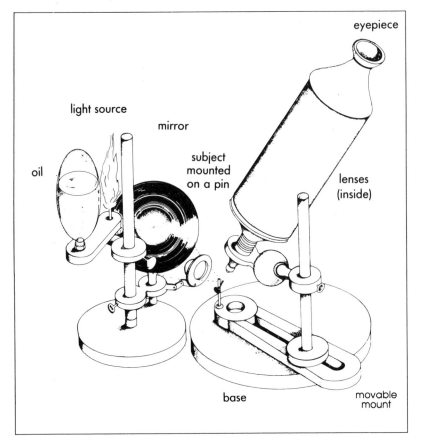

Fig. 4: With Leeuwenhoek's microscope, an oil lamp was used as a light source and the object to be viewed was mounted on a pin.

18

green ones, is protists. A protist is neither a plant nor an animal (not even a first animal) but rather a microscopic organism with a nucleus.

In 1683, after he had already seen many protists under the microscope, Leeuwenhoek discovered even smaller organisms, bacteria. Since many of the bacteria he observed could swim, he called them animals, but they certainly did not otherwise resemble animals, nor were they like plants. The discovery of the microscopic world was a major step toward the recognition that two kingdoms were not enough to describe all living beings.

Charles Darwin, Ernst Haeckel, and Problems With Taxonomy

Charles Darwin (1809–1892) observed that all organisms produce more offspring (more eggs, more puppies, more seeds, more pollen grains) than are able to survive. Only some offspring grow to maturity; the rest die from lack of food, attack by predators, or many other reasons. Darwin called this phenomenon—the survival of only a few of the many possible offspring—natural selection. Of all the possible offspring, those that live long enough to have offspring of their own survive because they are the best suited for the conditions around them.

Darwin also realized that individual offspring differ slightly from their parents and that these differences often occur because children inherit different traits from each parent. He reasoned that the accumulation of inherited differences over long periods of time would lead to the natural selection of descendant groups that were distinguishable as unique types stemming from the same original parents—as, for example, huskies, beagles, cocker spaniels, and collies, which all differ from their common wolflike ancestors.

In 1859, Darwin published *On the Origin of Species by Means of Natural Selection,* a book that gave numerous examples showing why he believed that species evolved. In addition to presenting Darwin's theory of evolution, this book revealed problems in Linnaeus' unchanging taxonomy. If all organisms came, as Darwin claimed they did, from a single common ancestor, was this ancestor a plant or an animal?

The German biologist Ernst Haeckel, who in the late nineteenth century defended Darwin's ideas on evolution, questioned the old taxonomy. Haeckel concluded that microbes, which were in his opinion more primitive than plants and animals, were the ancestors of all larger organisms. When he realized that microbes (bacteria and protists) were fundamentally different from plants and animals, he decided they needed a kingdom of their own. Haeckel called this kingdom Monera. During his lifetime he changed his mind several times about how organisms should be classified. Although he always put bacteria in the Kingdom Monera, he was not so sure about protists (such as amebas). Sometimes he included them, and sometimes he didn't.

Haeckel's confusion arose because many protists exhibit clear characteristics of both plants and animals, yet they are microbes. For example, the protist *Euglena gracilis* (Figure 5) has green parts that photosynthesize like leaves of a plant. It also swims and crawls (types of self-propulsion that are considered animal traits). Deciding into which kingdom to put *Euglena* was not easy.

Other odd organisms like *Euglena,* invisible to the unaided eye, were seen for the first time when the microscope was invented. Most were bigger than *Euglena,* but from the drawings made of these tiny living things, some must have been much smaller bacteria. Those that did not move (and were green or brownish) were called plants or algae, which means water plants. (All the living beings seen easily with a microscope are water-dwellers.) But many microscopic organisms, like *Euglena,* have both plant and animal characteristics. If whole-body movement makes an animal an animal, and photosynthesis makes a plant a plant, then what about the organisms that both photosynthesize and swim?

The purpose of classification systems is to be able to identify things and place them clearly into one category or another. The

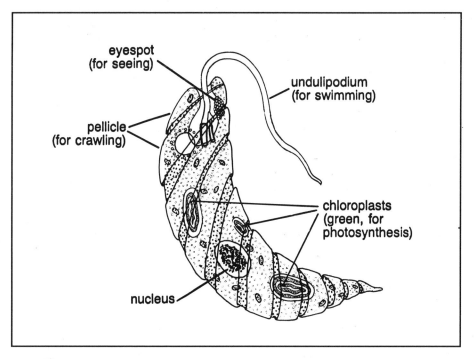

Fig. 5: *Euglena gracilis,* a common pond-water protist.

difficulty in categorizing *Euglena* might suggest that there is some-thing wrong with it, that it is a biological misfit; but the problem is not with *Euglena.* The problem is with the classification system itself. We realize now that, if organisms do not fit well into a taxonomic system, it is as much the fault of the system as it is of the organisms.

If there were only a few misfits, then the old system could be preserved, but the problem of classification has become major in recent years. There are hundreds of thousands of living beings that do not fit into the definition of plants as photosynthetic or that of animals as moving.

We now recognize many forms of life that are very different from both plants and animals. Many are far less like either plants or animals than *Euglena* is like both. But just because some living things do not fit neatly into one of these two kingdoms does not mean that these

21

organisms are unimportant. Some "misfits," such as diatoms and bacteria, are not really lower forms of life but rather are so important that those of us who consider ourselves higher forms of life could not exist without them.

Whittaker and the Five-Kingdom System

Haeckel's ideas were first adopted in the United States in 1956, when biologist H. P. Copeland (1902–1968) separated Haeckel's Monera kingdom into two separate kingdoms. He wrote a book presenting a four-kingdom classification of organisms—which almost no one read. Copeland's classification system included two kingdoms for microscopic beings—one for bacteria, the other for protists.

Copeland and other biologists realized that all organisms are made of cells either with or without nuclei. As microscopes improved, it became easier to detect the presence or absence of nuclei. Since all plants and animals have cells with nuclei, animal cells are much more like plant cells than they are like bacterial cells, which do not have nuclei.

By 1959 Cornell University Professor R. H. Whittaker (1924–1980) had read Copeland's book thoroughly and agreed with the two microbial kingdoms that Copeland proposed. In addition, while studying pine forests in New Jersey, Whittaker found that fungi, which never photosynthesize, were so unlike plants that he could no longer call them plants at all. Whittaker proposed the new five-kingdom system that biologists and teachers use today. His five-kingdom system describes the complexity of life much better than the old plant-versus-animal system. At the same time, it does not split life into so many different kingdoms that they are hard to remember.

We accept Whittaker's five kingdoms: (1) Monera (bacteria); (2) Protista (now called *Protoctista*; weird organisms including all large algae, amebas, and their relatives; they all have nuclei in their cells); (3) Fungi (molds, yeasts, and mushrooms); (4) Animalia (animals); and (5) Plantae (plants). These are the five major kinds of life on Earth (see page 6).

22

Three important biologists interested in the diversity and evolution of life. Ernst Haeckel (left) divided life into three kingdoms, Herbert Copeland (top right) made four, and Robert Whittaker (bottom right) established five kingdoms.

Whereas Whittaker included only single-celled organisms (protists) in the Kingdom Protoctista, we, like Copeland, also include their larger relatives. This allows us to group organisms together because of more important similarities than just size. For example, in our system, tiny green algae (which are protists) are together with their larger relatives, the green seaweeds. Both are considered protoctists (the informal name of members of the Kingdom Protoctista).

3

Kingdom Monera: Bacteria

The Kingdom Monera consists solely of bacteria, the life forms from which all other organisms come. Bacteria are so strange that, compared to other organisms, they seem like alien life forms. They are the tiniest living beings, so small that even by microscopic standards they seem like dwarfs; yet they eat, grow, excrete waste, respire, and reproduce like any other being. New techniques such as electron microscopy show that bacteria are very different not only from plants, animals, and fungi, but also from other microbes. Scientists put bacteria into their own kingdom because, unlike all other organisms, they lack nuclei in their cells (Figure 6).

The simplest and most limited bacteria are single, colorless, subvisible spheres or rods bounded by a flexible membrane (Figure 7). Although most bacteria have cell walls outside their membranes and many can swim, form seedlike structures (called spores), and photosynthesize (Figure 8), the simplest bacteria simply exchange gases and liquids. At the mercy of their environments, these bacteria cannot go anywhere unless they are pushed by water currents or winds or are carried by other living beings.

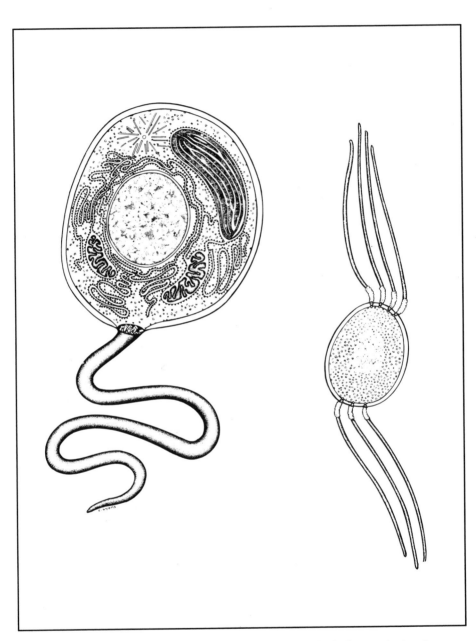

Fig. 6: Although both of these organisms can swim and both photosynthesize, the algal cell (left) is classified in the Kingdom Protoctista because it has a nucleus and other features of eukaryotes, whereas the bacterial cell (right) which lacks a nucleus, belongs to the Kingdom Monera.

What Are Bacteria?

All bacteria are united into one kingdom on the basis of their cell structure. They are called prokaryotes because their cells lack nuclei. (In Latin *pro* means "before", and *karyon* means "seed" or "nucleus.") Bacteria live almost everywhere: inside rocks, between sand grains in the desert, in scalding hot springs, and even high up in the stratosphere.

Bacteria are tough. Some can stand great heat, and others can survive being frozen in liquid nitrogen. As a group, bacteria can withstand more pressure, more drying out, and greater changing conditions of temperature and pressure than other life forms do.

Unlike animals, which come in two genders—male and female, bacteria do not have sexes. Bacteria reproduce asexually—one bacterium divides to become two. The "sex" of a bacterium changes rapidly. Even though bacteria do not have two genders that come together to make new bacteria, they do have a sex life. (Sex in biology means making a new, unique individual from the genes of one or more parents.)

The genes in a bacterium are dispersed throughout the inside of the cell. A bacterium receives new genes either from another bacterium or from bits of DNA floating in the water around it. Some bacteria can trade almost none of their genes, but other bacteria can trade almost all of their genes. Only the genes that are useful to the bacterium are retained. Copies of these new genes are made when-ever the bacterium reproduces.

Even bacteria that are genetically different from each other can trade genes. This ability makes bacteria different from all other organisms. A human cannot breed with a walrus, and no bird lays fish eggs, but different bacteria do take on each other's traits by genetic recombination. The kind of gene trading they do allows them to recombine different traits in a way that plants or animals never can. Of course, the traits inherited and exchanged by bacteria do not involve the presence of particular body parts such as wings or eyes, as in animals; instead, bacteria mix and match chemical abilities.

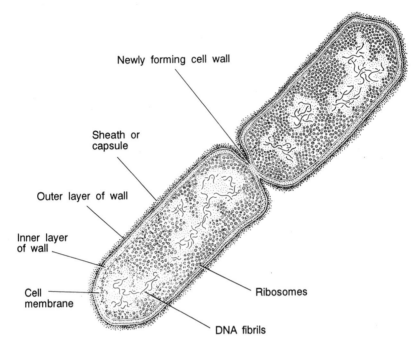

Fig. 7: *Bacteroides fragilis*, a rod-shaped bacterium (here shown reproducing by division).

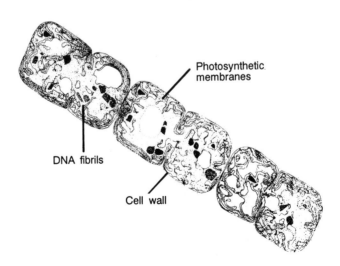

Fig. 8: *Anabaena*, multicellular filamentous blue-green bacterium that photosynthesizes.

Bacteria have been genetically engineering themselves by trading genes for billions of years; it is only recently that people have tapped into this ancient process. Laboratory technicians genetically engineer bacteria by implanting new genes in them. For example, some bacteria make chemicals that prevent ice crystals from forming at freezing temperatures. By inserting genes from these bacteria into bacteria that grow harmlessly on the surface of crop plants, people have been able to protect food crops from dying because of frost.

Diversity Within the Kingdom

About 20,000 kinds of chemically distinct bacteria have been identified. A spoonful of high-quality garden soil contains about 10,000 billion bacteria of hundreds of different kinds. Their ability to trade genes means that new kinds of bacteria come along all the time, and scientists are sure that many existing bacteria have not yet even been discovered. Since they are so small and so varied, bacteria are present in much greater numbers than any other kind of life on Earth. Although they have only a limited number of shapes (Figure 9), some bacteria come together to form multicellular structures (Figure 10). Many, maybe most, exist in some kind of multicellular form.

Major groups of bacteria include fermenters, sulfate reducers, photosynthesizers, and spirochetes. Fermenting bacteria do not use oxygen to obtain energy; they come from a time when there was no oxygen in Earth's atmosphere. They probably thrived on sugars and other food compounds found naturally on Earth shortly after life first evolved, as they still do. Fermenting bacteria live on milk sugar and are commonly found in milk and yogurt. Their overgrowth leads to souring, since they produce acid waste. These types of bacteria are used for many purposes—for example, to ferment juice to vinegar or wine, to make the flavor enhancer monosodium glutamate (MSG), and to produce cheese.

Sulfate reducers are a kind of bacteria that live in mud and soils. When they make and release chemicals like hydrogen sulfide, they cause odors like that of rotten eggs. Sulfate-reducing bacteria use one form of sulfur, called sulfate, and produce another form, called sulfide. Since all organisms on Earth need sulfur, and many can use it only in the form of sulfide, which is not readily available, these bacteria are important on a global scale. Fool's gold (iron sulfide) is produced when the smelly sulfur gases produced by these bacteria react with iron in the ground. *Thermoplasma* is a sulfur bacterium that lacks a cell wall and lives in water so hot, acidic, and full of sulfur that few other bacteria can survive to compete with it.

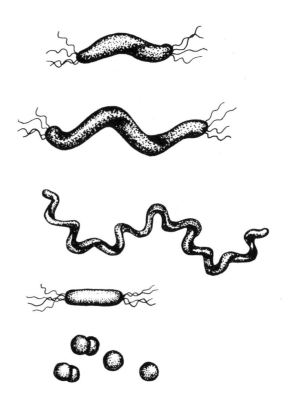

Fig. 9: Single-celled bacteria have shapes like these. From top to bottom: 1) vibrio, 2) spirillum, 3) spirochete, 4) rod or bacillus, and 5) cocci or spheres.

Fig. 10: This multicellular soil organism, called *Stigmatella,* is made of millions of single-celled bacteria.

The most productive way of life on Earth, photosynthesis, evolved in the earliest bacteria. Some photosynthetic bacteria live without food or oxygen; as long as they have light, carbon dioxide, hydrogen sulfide, and salt water, they live, reproduce, and therefore keep their type in existence forever.

Spirochetes (Figure 11) are wriggling bacteria that can be found in many places, including clams and oysters—and even on the tongue. The fastest swimmers in the bacterial world, spirochetes often are found propelling other bacteria around; they act like natural motors.

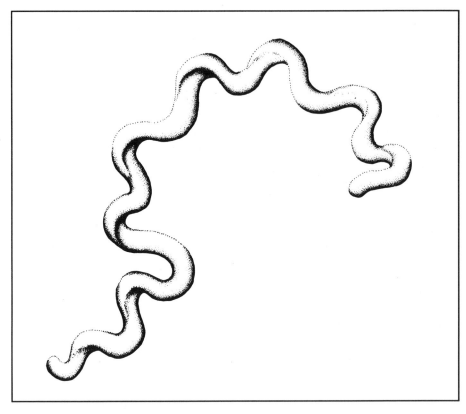

Fig. 11: Spirochetes are bacteria that wriggle, bend, and swim toward things they like, and away from things they don't like.

Only a few of the major groups of bacteria are mentioned here. Even though you cannot see them without using a microscope, these members of the oldest kingdom are everywhere on the surface of our planet. Billions of years ago some bacteria evolved into the protoctists, the first cells with nuclei. We discuss protoctists in the next chapter.

Some Effects of Bacteria on Other Organisms

Scientists agree that the earliest living beings on Earth were bacteria. All life comes ultimately from bacteria. Bacteria have lived all over Earth—in moist soils, ponds, seas, and elsewhere—ever since life began some three-and-one-half billion years ago. Only in the last one-fifth of life's existence on Earth have living forms evolved that are not bacteria. The more recent organisms—plants, animals, protoctists, and fungi—contain cell parts called organelles that are very similar to certain bacteria. These organelles probably were bacteria at one time. Many bacteria are symbiotic, which means that they live together with or even inside of other organisms for most of their lives. For some bacteria this kind of coexistence (symbiosis) leads them to become part of the same cells in which they live.

Bacteria are chemically amazing; they release into the atmosphere and remove from it all of its major reactive gases. By releasing oxygen, as well as various forms of carbon gases, and taking up nitrogen gas, bacteria play the major role in Earth's recycling of sulfur, nitrogen, and other chemical elements.

Although bacteria are often thought of as bad germs, the truth is that most of them are environmental good guys; bacteria break down toxins, circulate gases, and, in general, keep planet Earth livable for other kinds of life. One reason people think bacteria are dangerous is because they multiply so fast. When their growth is not limited by food or water (that is, when the supply of food and water is so plentiful that the bacteria can get as much as they can possibly take in), bacteria can "bloom": one divides to become two, two split to become four, four become eight, and so on at an alarming rate. In a few days, one well-supplied bacterium could grow to be a bacterial colony the size and weight of Earth!

Of course, there are never enough available nutrients for this to happen. Nonetheless, the ability of bacteria to grow very fast can be dangerous for nearby organisms that provide the bacteria with food and water. Growing unchecked inside the bodies of other organisms, bacteria can cause disease. Tuberculosis, leprosy, bubonic plague, strep throat, skin infections, and many other diseases involve growing bacteria.

Since the human body usually functions in harmony with its bacteria, very few bacterial diseases actually kill. The bacterium

Escherichia coli is normally found in the human gut and aids digestion. Animals need bacteria to digest their food. Cows, who have four stomachs, require many kinds of bacteria to digest grass, breaking down the cellulose of grass into sugars, hydrogen, and carbon dioxide in the cow's rumen (the first of its four stomachs). Certain bacteria grow well in the presence of the hydrogen and carbon dioxide in this special stomach. These bacteria, called methanogens, produce the gas methane, which is belched out in large quantities by the cow.

Indeed, much of the methane in Earth's atmosphere comes from methane-making bacteria, including those in the stomachs of elephants, buffalo, and cows. Termites also have swollen intestines full of bacteria. Some of the methane of the air comes from bacteria in termite intestines. Without these bacteria, termites would not be able to digest their food, wood. Most bacteria in nature are not disease-causing germs but rather natural parts of the larger organisms they inhabit.

If long-lasting stations are built in space, many kinds of bacteria will be brought along to keep the soil of these space stations fertile and the air inside them clean. Bacteria will be needed for the growth of the garden vegetables that will be part of the space dwellers' diets. Bacteria will help recycle sewage and garbage. They will help break down animal (including human) waste to supply nutrients for plants and algae. Taking advantage of the ease with which bacteria acquire new genes, scientists now are developing new forms of bacteria that can clean up oil spills and recycle plastics.

Modified bacteria produce medicines quickly and cheaply. By implanting certain genes into bacteria—for example, genes for the compound insulin—important life-saving medicines are made. Normal insulin is produced naturally in most people, but it is missing from people with the disease diabetes. Until recently, insulin needed by diabetics was extracted from cows, an expensive process. However, human insulin can be "manufactured" much more cheaply by injecting human genes for insulin into bacteria. The bacteria grow rapidly in the laboratory, producing insulin that is better than that extracted from cows because it is actually human insulin. The genetic engineering of bacteria is thus the only feasible way to make human insulin in significant quantities.

Although some people talk about bacteria as though they were enemy agents out to harm us and spoil our food, this is a shortsighted view. Bacteria keep our soil fertile and our air and water clean. The first kingdom of life, they are as essential to our well-being now as they were to the evolution of our ancestors.

4

Kingdom Protoctista: Euglenas, Amebas, and Their Larger Relatives With Nuclei

When people believed that all life fit into only two kingdoms, algae (such as seaweed) were considered to be plants and amebas were considered to be animals; but algae and amebas are really neither plants nor animals. Now we recognize both as protoctists. The microscopic world is full of all sorts of protoctists—small ones (protists) like paramecia, amebas, and euglenas and large ones like slime nets that are even more unusual. Furthermore, new protoctists are being discovered far faster than new animals or plants these days.

Protoctist refers to every member of this kingdom—from tiny transparent amebas to huge brown kelps and yellow slime molds. Protist refers only to the microscopic members.

Protoctists developed when different kinds of bacteria, each with different abilities, came together into symbiotic, or physically associated, relationships over one billion years ago and formed the first cells with nuclei. This event was very significant because these protoctists, the first life forms with nuclei, became the ancestors of all other life forms—plants, animals, and fungi. Ancient green algae, like the modern one in Figure 12, were ancestors of herbs, trees, and shrubs. Ancient, transparent protoctists were ancestors of the yeasts, mushrooms, and molds that recycle dead organisms back into the soil and air. Scientists debate which ancient protoctists were ancestral to animals; no one is sure.

What Are Protoctists?

Like animals, plants, and fungi, all protoctists are eukaryotes (from *eu* meaning "true," and *karyon*, meaning "kernel" or "nucleus"); that is, they have at least one nucleus, and many have other cell parts, called

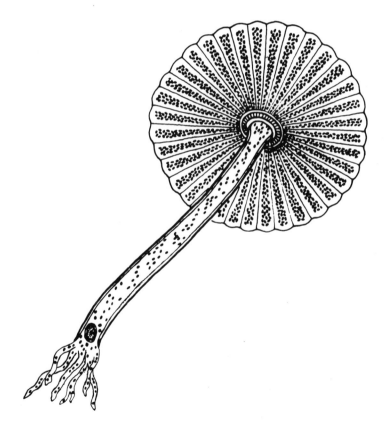

Fig. 12: *Acetabularia*, a green alga that grows on rocks in the Mediterranean Sea.

organelles. (Bacteria are the only organisms that do not have nuclei.) Organelles are tiny structures that are the organs of the cell, like internal organs in animals. Inside the tiny green spheres of the protist *Chlorella,* for example, are organelles called chloroplasts and mitochondria. Photosynthesis occurs in chloroplasts, and respiration (the process of getting energy using oxygen) occurs in mitochondria.

All protoctists live in water (either salt water or fresh water). Sometimes this water is within the watery tissues of other organisms. Protoctists may be photosynthetic (making their own food from sunlight and gases in the air) or nonphotosynthetic (eating food that is already available). They all grow, excrete waste, exchange gases, and reproduce. The simplest protoctists are single, spherical, colorless cells—like some soil amebas.

Some protoctists cannot reproduce sexually; they simply divide into two new parts. Others have an extremely complex sex life. For example, some change their sex every dusk and every dawn: they are one sex during the middle of the day, another in the middle of the night, and no sex at all at twilight. These protoctists have to mate every few weeks, or they will die. Furthermore, although two organisms of opposite sex come together for the mating act, the act itself produces no offspring; it just renews, refreshes, and invigorates the organisms. (This is because sex for them involves exchanging nuclei.) Unlike all plants and animals, no protoctist forms an embryo.

Diversity Within the Kingdom

Protoctists make up a great realm of organisms, far more diverse than animals and plants. Some of the more well-known protoctists are slime molds, malarial parasites, paramecia, amebas, red tide organisms, diatoms, brown seaweeds, pond scum, euglenas, potato-blight organisms, kelps, and green seaweeds. This is a very short list; it is suspected that there are more than 250,000 different species of protoctists! Protoctists inhabit all the waters of the world.

Members of this kingdom vary incredibly in size. The smallest examples (protists) have only one or just a few cells; the largest are gigantic. The largest known protoctists are the giant kelps off the coast of the state of Washington. These brown algae, which can be 100 feet long, have heavy, sticky holdfasts (structures for attachment) that bind them to rocks in the crashing surf.

Protoctists are varied in many other ways besides size: ciliates swim, slime molds form spores, and pond weeds form branched structures. Although some protoctists are at the mercy of their environments and cannot go anywhere unless they are moved passively by water currents, winds, or other living beings, others use oarlike structures to propel themselves through the water.

A number of truly astonishing traits exist among organisms within this kingdom. There are many kinds of amebas—protists whose shape is constantly changing (Figure 13). The giant ameba, for example, looks like a wine flask and has hundreds of nuclei in its cells. One of the few protoctists that is poisoned by too much oxygen, it probably has changed very little from its ancestral form compared to other protoctists. Indeed, the giant ameba may be similar to the kinds of life that prevailed when the first protoctists evolved from bacteria some two billion years ago.

Sea whirlers—technically called dinomastigotes or dinoflagellates—live in the ocean (Figure 14). Some of them are responsible for red tides, which occur when the conditions are right for these sea whirlers to "bloom" (just like bacteria bloom when food and water are plentiful). The ocean actually looks red because so many of these red sea whirlers are present. Fish who eat them become poisonous, and humans can die from eating the poisoned fish.

Other sea whirlers glow in the dark, especially when shaken. Still others live symbiotically in corals, clams, or sea anemones, assisting in the construction of great reefs under the water. Some dinomastigotes even have colored membranes sensitive to light that form a kind of eye.

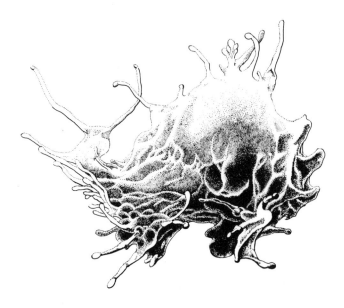

Fig. 13: An ameba as seen with the scanning electron microscope. In life, amebas are always moving and changing.

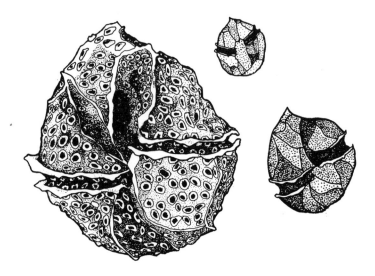

Fig. 14: Sea whirlers (or dinomastigotes). The swimming forms convert into these hard-walled forms (cysts) that drop to the sea bottom.

The white cliffs of Dover in England were built by chalk-making protists called coccolithophorids. (In Greek, *cocco* means "berry-shaped," *litho* means "stone," and *phora* means "to carry," so they are very well named!) The little coccoliths piled up over thousands of years to help form these white cliffs, which were exposed when the level of the ocean dropped. These same life forms produce the gas dimethyl sulfide, which makes the sea smell like the sea. Their blooms can be seen from satellites (Figure 15).

The diatoms, another kind of protist, are among the most beautiful organisms on Earth, yet they can be seen only with a microscope. Diatoms are made of silica, the main material of opals, rubies, petrified wood, sand,

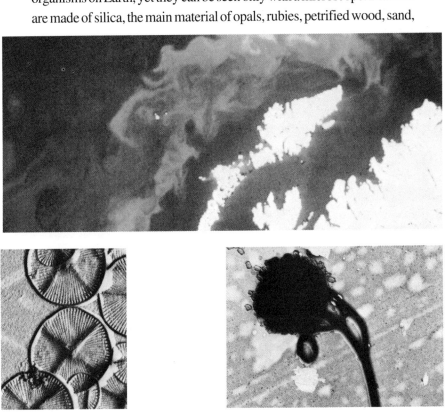

Fig. 15: Protoctists from space: a great bloom of colored water (above) seen from a satellite west of the islands off the coast of Scotland. Millions of scaly algae (lower right) have shed their white chalky scales (lower left) into the water.

sand, and glass (Figure 16). Like plants and other algae, diatoms get their energy to make food by photosynthesis.

Perhaps the weirdest protoctists are the slime nets, like *Labyrinthula* (Figure 17), and the slime molds, of which there are several major groups. Reminiscent of creatures in low-budget science fiction films, slime molds have been found oozing across golf courses or leaving tracks of slime across wooden tables and drawers in laboratories.

The amazing thing about some slime molds is that they are really amebas that congregate to form a new being. One species of slime mold is composed of individual amebas that live apart in the soil. When the

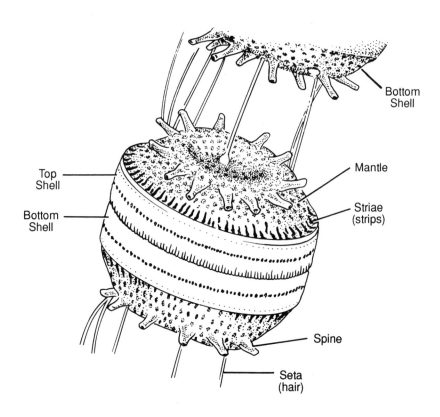

Fig. 16: A diatom, showing its finely sculptured shell made of silica.

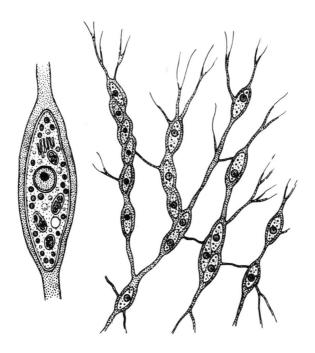

Fig. 17: *Labyrinthula* (right) is a slime-net organism that lives on the leaves of eel grass in the ocean. Enlarged at left is one cell surrounded by the slime it made.

amebas run out of food, they release a chemical that signals them all to come together, like football players into a huddle. What were once individual amebas then become a single organism, growing upward into a "spore tower." Eventually the spore tower, which looks like a miniature tree, dries out. Winds come along and blow its spores far and wide. When moistened, the spores come to life again as individual amebas.

Some Effects of Protoctists on Other Organisms
Familiar protoctists include the photosynthetic organisms in lakes, streams, and oceans. When they float in water, often serving as food for fish, shrimp, and other aquatic animals, they are called plankton. (Some of the planktonic protoctists you may have heard of are diatoms

and green algae.) When they are attached to the bottom of the body of water in which they live, photosynthetic protoctists are called benthic algae. Benthic algae, such as green and red seaweeds, provide food for oysters, snails, clams, and other salt-water organisms that are important to humans as seafood.

Certain protoctists cause illnesses—especially in the tropics—such as malaria and sleeping sicknesses. But most are indirectly helpful in the environment (as food for fish and other marine organisms or in the preparation of soil) or even directly to us (as red algae used in ice cream preparation). The diversity in structure and sex lives of protoctists is still poorly known; many surprises are in store for the curious.

5

Kingdom Fungi: Yeasts, Molds, and Mushrooms

The Kingdom Fungi is made up of yeasts, molds, and mushrooms. Although they come from thready protoctists, no one knows their ancestry for sure. The smallest are tiny cells, and the largest are huge mushrooms. The largest fungi that scientists know of is a common mold called *Armillaria bulbosa*, discovered in Crystal Falls, Michigan. This one organism is so large, it is said to weigh 100 tons! It is also very old; scientists speculate that it has been growing since the last Ice Age. It may even be the oldest organism on Earth today. However, most fungi are not so large. In fact, we need microscopes to see what they really are like.

What Are Fungi?

Even before microbes were discovered, fungi posed a problem for the traditional two-kingdom classification system. An ancient Arabian book described fungi as being midway between the mineral and plant kingdoms. A mushroom rooted in the ground may at first appear to be a kind of plant, but fungi, which include mushrooms as well as the green mold that grows on damp bread, are very different from plants. Plants derive their energy and food from sunlight. Fungi, however, can thrive in the dark. Fungi do not photosynthesize (photosynthesis is from the Greek words for light and making).

Instead, all fungi absorb their food directly from their surroundings—the soil, the insides of a rotting log, or the damp material of an old piece of bread. (Unlike animals, fungi digest food outside rather than inside their bodies by releasing enzymes onto their food and rotting it.) This peculiar earthiness of fungi is probably what convinced the writers of the Arabian work that fungi were only half alive—that is, midway between nonliving minerals and living plants. Fungi, like microbes, are misfits in the old two-kingdom classification system.

Unlike both animals and plants, fungi do not form embryos. Rather, every fungus—whether yeast, mold, or mushroom—grows from tiny powdery cells called spores. Fungal spores are specially adapted survival structures that are resistant to drying out, cold, and other extreme conditions that would normally inhibit the growth of or even kill the growing cells of molds, mushrooms, and yeasts.

Diversity Within the Kingdom

There are three major types of fungi: mating molds (called zygofungi), sac fungi (called ascofungi), and club fungi (called basidiofungi).

Zygofungi include the black molds that rot fruit left out in a bowl too long. Although zygofungi reproduce by spores, the spores can be produced either sexually or without sex. Sexual mating results in special tubes whose ends "kiss" (Figure 18). The tubes grow together to form a dark sporehead, which fills with spores. A gust of wind blows the spores away. When the spores land on damp places, they grow into a new mold, ready to mate again. A single stalk can produce spores asexually—that is, without mating first. Spores simply grow off the top and float away in the air.

Molds look like white, green, or peach-colored fuzzy material or like brown spots on food. To grow common bread mold, simply leave a piece of bakery bread (without preservatives) in a plastic bag to keep

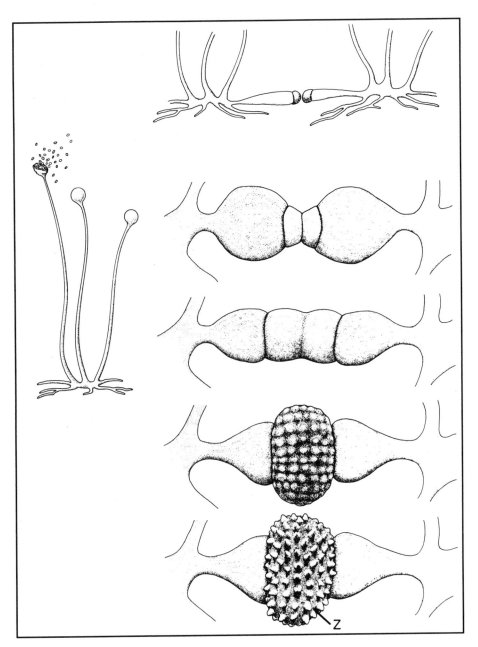

Fig. 18: A black bread mold, *Rhizopus*, reproduces by spores (left). When opposite mating types contact (right), they form this hard black structure called a zygospore (z).

it from drying out. The black moist spots that form in a couple of days most likely will include the bread mold fungus *Rhizopus stolonifer.* The mold absorbs the same sugar and starch that people like to eat. Molds also thrive on horse dung, which provides them with cellulose, nitrogen, and other nutrients found in animal waste. Fungi are crucial to recycling: they consume hair, corn, coffee grounds, film, skin, cotton, feathers, and wood. Rotting logs on the forest floor are a very good place to scout for fungi.

Ascofungi include brewer's yeast and baker's yeast, as well as morels and truffles (two kinds of mushrooms), and pink bread molds. Fungi of this sort produce spores inside an ascus, a special sac that is observed easily with a microscope. Among the ascofungi are found many of the annoying organisms that cause disease. Some of these maladies, such as athlete's foot and ringworm, occur because certain ascofungi are able to digest keratin, the protein found in hair, skin, and nails.

Lichens (Figure 19) are actually symbioses, or physical associations, between ascofungi and green algae or photosynthesizing bacteria. The photosynthesizing bacteria provide the nutrients required for the lichen to survive, and the ascofungi protect the bacteria from environmental extremes. This mutually beneficial relationship allows lichens, which resemble moss or other simple plants, to grow on tree bark and rocks, environments that would normally be too harsh for the bacteria to survive.

The last major type of fungi is the basidiofungi (Figure 20). These include smuts, jelly fungi, rusts, stinkhorns, and the common supermarket variety of mushroom with the scientific name *Agaricus campestris* (field mushroom). Basidiofungi produce spores in a club-shaped organ called a basidium. Many basidiofungi digest wood; among these fungi are the chanterelles, the horn of plenty, dry-rot fungi, paint fungi, bracket fungi, tooth fungi, and coral fungi. The destroying angel mushroom, *Amanita phalloides,* is a deadly mushroom related to the mind-altering *Amanita muscaria* and the delicious

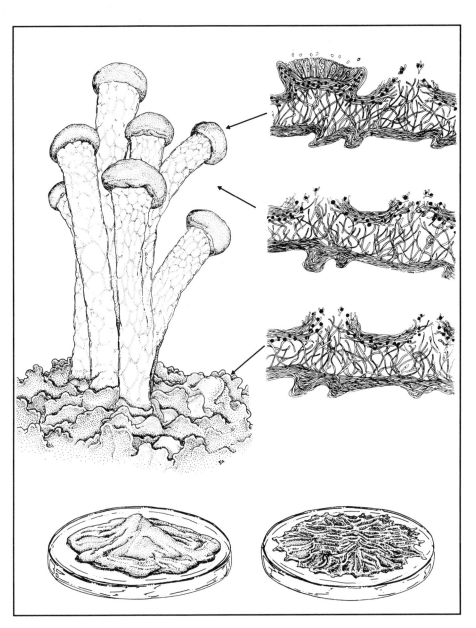

Fig. 19: The British soldier lichen, at left, is a symbiont composed of a fungus (shown growing alone or on a petri plate, lower left) and a green alga (shown growing alone or on a petri plate, lower right). The inner details of the relation between the fungal thread and the algal balls as seen with a microscope are shown at upper right. The arrows point to the part of the lichen from which the sample was taken.

Fig. 20: *Pholiota terrestris*, a common woodland mushroom.

Amanita caesarea; although related to each other, even very similar-looking mushrooms can have very different consequences once they are eaten. Most of the edible mushrooms are basidiofungi. Among these are the fairy-ring mushroom, used as a spice when dried; the shiitake mushroom, used in Japanese cooking; and cloud, or tree-ear, mushrooms, often found in Chinese food.

Some Effects of Fungi on Other Organisms
Many people are afraid of fungi because they think they are strange, possibly poisonous organisms. Mushrooms—the most well-known fungi—have long been associated with witchcraft, and some hallucinogenic drugs, like psilocybin, come from mushrooms. Many mushrooms are poisonous, but others are completely harmless and

edible. Other fungi cause athlete's foot and jock itch and can make sneakers smell bad, but they are not poisonous.

Many fungi, in fact, have beneficial properties. Champagne, wine, and beer are produced by fermentation carried on by yeasts. Other kinds of these single-celled fungi make bread rise and give it its spongy texture (Figure 21). Fungi ripen fine cheeses such as Brie and Camembert, and they flavor soy sauce. Along with plants, fungi may have been the first organisms to move to land some 450 million years ago. Since they bring necessary nutrients to some plants and allow forests to grow, even this piece of paper may exist because of the relationship between trees and fungi. The tree-feeding mushroom on the forest floor can be traced underground by its fine threads to the roots of the tree to which the threads are attached.

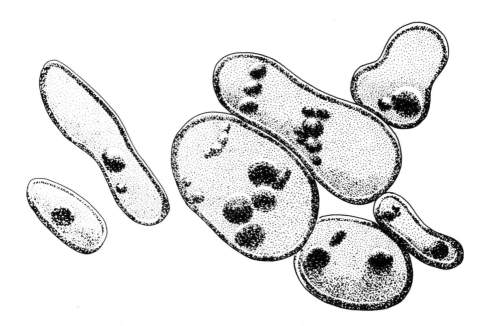

Fig. 21: Cells of *Saccharomyces,* as seen with a high-power microscope. This is the yeast we use in baking bread and brewing beer.

Penicillium chrysogenum (Figure 22), a mold that grows on breads, produces penicillin, an antibiotic that works by preventing the growth of the cell walls of bacteria. Use of the drug penicillin has saved hundreds of thousands of human lives from death by bacterial infection. The blue-green veins in Roquefort cheese are produced by a different *Penicillium* species, a fungus that lacks sex but in which any of its threads can reproduce itself by forming spores.

A world without fungi would be so crowded with dead bodies that no room would be left. Fungi are essential to soil-making and element-recycling, especially on forested land, where they supplement bacterial activities. Fungi attached to roots bring phosphate and other fertilizers to trees. Without their activities, we would starve and have no fresh air to breathe.

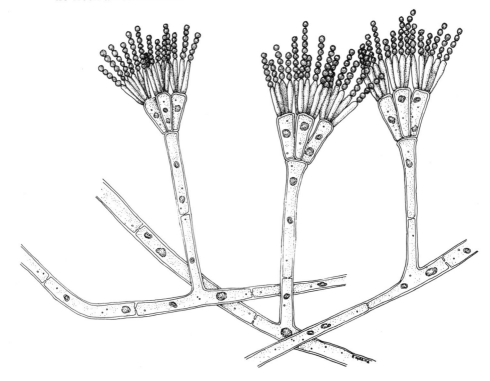

Fig. 22: The greenish fuzz of *Penicillium*, the common mold, looks like this with a high-power microscope. The round spores are green.

6

Kingdom Animalia: Animals

Protozoa used to be called one-celled animals because they were not plants. In the five-kingdom system, however, there is no such thing as a one-celled animal. (We now realize that what used to be considered one-celled animals differ greatly from animals, so they are classified as protoctists.) Most scientists agree that animals evolved from protoctists, but no one knows which kind of protoctists were ancestors to the first animals.

What Are Animals?

The Kingdom Animalia includes fish, birds, reptiles, mammals, and insects. These living things are alike in that they are composed of many cells, they exhibit complex behavior, and they reproduce from a structure called a blastula. The blastula is a small, hollow ball of cells produced when a sperm fertilizes and merges with an egg (Figure 23). The multicellular blastula, which later becomes the young animal, forms as the fertilized cell divides.

Some members of other kingdoms, especially some protoctists, share animal traits (like having many cells and behaving in complex ways), but these traits exist more strongly in the Kingdom Animalia.

One example of complex behavior that exists only among animals is flying. Insects, bats, and birds all are able to fly; even some dinosaurs flew. No organisms besides animals are capable of this complex behavior.

Animals have a wide variety of eating habits. Some—like spiders, lions, and eagles—are carnivorous (meat-eating); they prey upon other animals for food. Others—like cows, rabbits, and termites—are herbivorous (plant-eating). Still other animals, including humans, are omnivorous; they eat both meat and plants. Although animals exhibit many different eating behaviors, very few are capable of manufacturing their own food, like most plants and many bacteria and protoctists are.

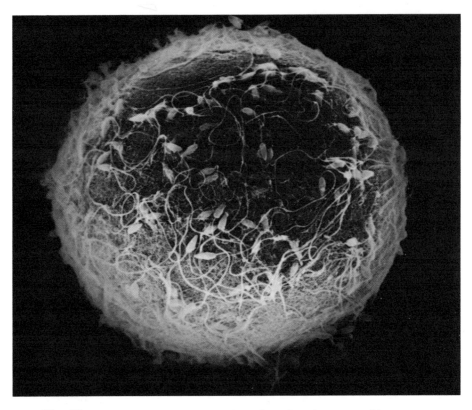

Fig. 23: Many small sperm surround the surface of one large sea urchin egg.

Diversity Within the Kingdom

The Kingdom Animalia consists of thirty-two different phyla, each containing thousands of organisms that share certain traits. Here we describe only a few of the more well-known phyla.

Dogs, cats, giraffes, whales, dinosaurs, fish, and frogs, among many others, are all called chordates because they have backbones. Inside the backbone is a nerve cord (called the spinal cord) running from the base of the brain down the length of the body. There are some 45,000 species of chordates, including a wide variety of organisms ranging from fish to humans. Many people think just of chordates when they think of animals, but chordates represent only one phylum of animal life. (Remember that a phylum is a much bigger category than species but is still smaller than a kingdom; see the table on page 16.)

The arthropods (animals with jointed legs), which are distinguished by segmented bodies and segmented limbs, are, after the backboned animals, most familiar to people. They have a hard external skeleton called an exoskeleton. All insects are arthropods, as are crustaceans, such as lobsters, shrimp, crayfish, crabs, and even barnacles. Insects are only one class in the phylum Arthropoda, just as mammals are only one class in the phylum Chordata. There are millions of species within this phylum; almost every day new insects are discovered in tropical areas like the South American rain forests. Arthropods are very important to plants, since many flowering plants depend on insects to fertilize them.

Coelenterates, another animal phylum, include *Hydra* (the tentacle-waving tube) and jellyfish. Coelenterates are carnivores that sting their prey with tentacles (Figure 24). They are round and use the hole in the center of their body both as a mouth and an anus (the opening from which waste is excreted).

Most groups of animals (twenty-nine out of thirty-two phyla) are sea-dwelling creatures of one kind or another. They are not all put together into one phylum for the same reason that Aristotle did not group dolphins together with fish: a detailed examination shows that

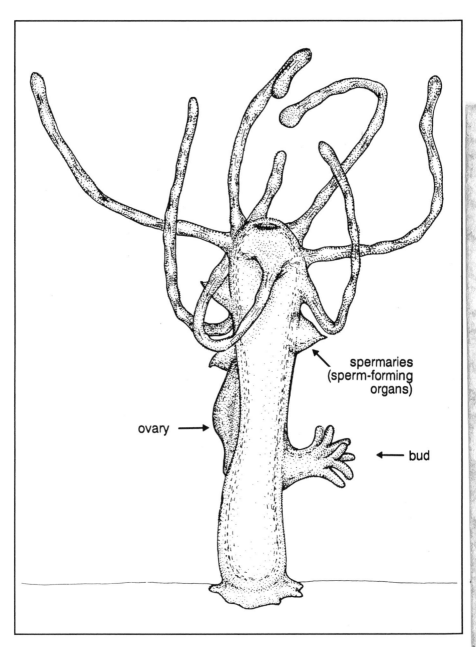

Fig. 24: *Hydra*, an animal with tentacles, is capable of "budding" off immature hydras every day.

their similarities are mostly on the surface. Flat worms, ribbon worms, jaw worms, and gastrotichs each have their own phylum containing many different species. Rotifers (wheel animals) are tiny marine animals, some only four-hundredths of a millimeter in length—as small as protists. Nonetheless, they are animals because they develop from a fertilized egg and a blastula.

Another phylum in the animal kingdom, called lamp shells or brachiopods, has only about 260 species in existence today. Their name comes from the fact that they are shaped like Aladdin's lamp. Some 30,000 species of brachiopods are extinct. We know of these extinct species because brachiopods have shells that survive as fossils.

The phylum of mollusks contains such familiar animals as clams, oysters, and other two-shelled shellfish. Some of the ancestors of these mollusks had only one shell. The existence of these live, one-shelled mollusks was discovered only recently, though their remains were uncovered in great quantity in the fossil record. In the late 1970s, California Institute of Technology professor Heinz Lowenstam examined the contents of a box core (a box made of wire mesh that is used to take samples of sediment from the ocean floor) that had been suspended in the water off Los Angeles, California, for one to two days. He found a "living fossil"—a living mollusk that had only one flat shell, just like its extinct ancestors.

The most famous members of the echinoderm phylum are starfish and sea urchins, but the group contains about 6,000 related species, all ocean dwellers. Many echinoderms can regenerate their body parts, and even their whole body, if damaged or destroyed.

The echiurans, commonly called spoon worms, are odd-looking marine worms with fat trunks and long, twisted snouts; they dwell in mud or the cracks of rocks.

Tardigrades are called waterbears (Figure 25). These organisms survive difficult conditions; some live in hot springs, others in the arctic snows. The biggest tardigrades are only 1–2 millimeters across—scarcely visible to the naked eye.

Poriferans, or sponges, a simple kind of animal, evolved separately from a kind of protist called a choanomastigote. Sponges consist of cell colonies that recognize each other so specifically that, if an adult sponge is squeezed through a filter, causing it to break apart, the cells will come back together, reforming the sponge in the water below. All other animals seem to have come from at least one other line of protoctists different from the ancestors that evolved into sponges.

Because we are mammals, we are fascinated with our mammal relatives and think that most animals are four-legged land dwellers that care for their young. This is not true. By far, most animals on land are beetles, and many in the sea are strange beasts that have no common names. The greatest diversity of animals is in the sea. The smallest animals are a fraction of an inch, and the largest, the blue

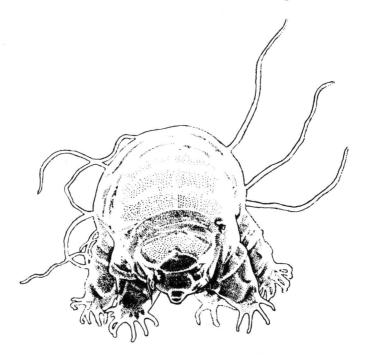

Fig. 25: "Waterbears" are small aquatic animals that are not bears at all; they are called tardigrades.

whales, are 100 meters long. Most animals are unknown except to the zoologists who study them.

Some Effects of Animals on Other Organisms

Animals greatly affect the population of photosynthesizing organisms because they require photosynthetic organisms either directly or indirectly for food. Animals limit the population growth of photosynthetic organisms (photosynthetic bacteria, algae, and plants) by eating them and therefore are agents of natural selection. Animals also affect the growth of individual photosynthesizers by supplying nitrogen-rich fertilizer (nitrogen is essential for growth) to plants and algae in the form of waste products—urine and feces.

Birds, bats, and insects are crucial in the life of flowering plants, most of which need to be pollinated before they can produce seeds. Bees seeking nectar from flowers, for example, transport pollen from the male parts (stamens) to the female parts (ovaries) of apple blossoms. Without the aid of animals in delivering pollen to the ovaries, the flower would not be fertilized, and no seeds or fruit would develop. (From a botanist's viewpoint, fruits such as apples, plums, cherries, and even tomatoes and bean pods are really the swollen walls of the ovary—the female part of the flower after it has been fertilized by the male pollen.)

Animals also play an important role in spreading plant seeds so that new generations of plants can develop. By eating and digesting only the outer coverings of seeds and then depositing the seeds in their feces, or by unknowingly carrying seeds as burrs in their fur, animals disperse the seeds of plants. Mammals, such as mice and squirrels, that bury seeds like acorns, corn, and grass seeds to keep them for winter usually store many more seeds than they actually need to survive and in so doing act as farmers who plant seeds far away from the parent plants.

Thus, animals play an important role in regulating the population of the organisms that make up their food, plants.

7

Kingdom Plantae: Plants

Like animals, plants evolved from protoctists. The first animals evolved earlier than the first plants, yet plants moved to land before animals did. Algae, especially green seaweeds, are thought to be ancestors of plants. One thousand million years ago algae dwelled in sunny shallow places. When these sunny shallow places dried up, most algae died. Some tough water-holding kinds were able to stay dry on the outside and wet on the inside. This was a crucial trick for growing on damp or dry land. So the first true plants did not live in water; they were waterproof, land-dwelling plants without stems or leaves.

What Are Plants?

In the five-kingdom system, Kingdom Plantae consists of those many-celled, tissue-forming organisms that develop from both spores and embryos. All plants are sexual organisms that grow from a tiny young being called an embryo. The embryo forms after a sperm (a cell with an undulipodium, called the sperm tail) made by a male plant fertilizes an egg made by a female plant. The fertile egg, which develops into the embryo, always remains attached to the female parent. The embryo has two sets of chromosomes, one from its egg-making mother and one from its sperm-forming father.

The embryo grows into a mature plant, called a sporophyte. Eventually the sporophyte produces tiny powdery bodies called spores. Each spore (which is produced by meiosis) grows into another mature plant, called a gametophyte if it survives. Gametophytes are either male (those that produce sperm again) or female (those that produce eggs). Generations alternate between sporophytes (spore-producing plants) and gametophytes (egg/sperm-producing plants), and this "alternation of generations" is characteristic of all plants, from tiny mosses to giant redwood trees.

In mosses, brown spores are carried on a stalk; they blow around and then land and grow on moist ground. In redwood trees, the seeds form inside the cone. Inside the seeds are embryos. The embryos of early plants, like today's mosses (Figure 26), developed from eggs that were fertilized by two-tailed sperm . The fact that the sperm of both plants and

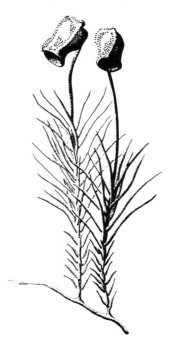

Fig. 26: *Polytrichum juniperum* is a common moss that lives in damp, shady forests.

animals have the same kind of tails (undulipodia) shows that plants and animals have more in common than you might think.

The great majority of plants are photosynthetic. Photosynthesis, the process in which the energy of sunlight and carbon dioxide gas (CO_2) from the atmosphere are converted into food (organic compounds—that is, compounds containing carbon), is what supports all life on Earth. Photosynthesis requires pigments (colored compounds) called chlorophylls, all of which are green. A few plants, like dodder or Indian pipe, form flowers with embryos and seeds and therefore are classified as plants, but they cannot photosynthesize because they lack chlorophyll and are whitish or orangish instead of green. Instead of photosynthesizing, they obtain food from other plants by attaching rootlike structures directly to their green neighbors. The green pigment chlorophyll is contained inside chloroplasts, which came originally from photosynthesizing bacteria. All plants have plastids in their cells—either green chloroplasts or white plastids, some of which may grow into chloroplasts.

In the process of photosynthesis, which occurs inside the chloroplasts, plants take in carbon dioxide gas in the presence of light. As long as plenty of water (H_2O) is also present, carbon atoms from the carbon dioxide combine with hydrogen atoms from the water to form sugars, starch, and other food molecules that have the general chemical formula, $C_nH_{2n}O_n$. Glucose, with the formula $C_6H_{12}O_6$, is an example. The oxygen atoms left over after the hydrogen atoms are removed from the water molecules combine to form oxygen gas (O_2)—the gas that all animals breathe.

Diversity Within the Kingdom

On land, plants evolved tough, hard cell-wall materials, called lignin and cellulose, which we know as wood. These hard substances allow trees and shrubs to stand erect without falling down. Early plants had flattened branches that were the first leaves. Water taken up from the soil by the roots was transported upward, and food manufactured in the leaves by photosynthesis was transported downward via a system of vessels. These plants with food- and water-conducting tubes are called the vascular plants. Some looked very much like today's *Psilotum* (Figure 27) and were thriving by 400 million years ago.

Living in the dry, hostile environment of the land was as difficult for plants as going to the moon is for humans. Seeds evolved as a way for plants to survive the harsh sunlight and drying winds. Seeds sprouted only when the surroundings were sufficiently wet from rain; if it was not wet, the seeds just waited until it was. Plants evolved from algae into many different sizes and shapes—from the seed ferns that formed a major part of the diet of dinosaurs to all the angiosperms, the great group of flowering plants ranging from dandelions to oak trees. No matter how different two plants may appear—a nonphotosynthetic Indian pipe and a

Fig. 27: *Psilotum* is an unusual plant that grows at the base of trees in Florida.

photosynthetic cactus, for example—somewhere inside them you will find cells corresponding to ancestral spores and embryos. Remains from an ancient past, they mark definitively the right to membership in the Plant Kingdom.

Some Effects of Plants on Other Organisms

We have already talked about the importance of photosynthesis to the survival of other organisms. Without plants, most organisms, including humans, could not exist. Plants produce food for all life on land, including members of all other kingdoms of life—protoctists, bacteria, fungi, and animals. They also supply shelter, fiber, and oxygen gas. As habitat-providers, plants have no equals.

Animals such as bats and bees, while feeding on nectar, fertilize flowers so that they can make their seeds. Without seeds we would have no fruits like apples, pears, or plums. Our lives depend on seeds of wheat for bread and those of barley for beer. Wood, rope, linen, cotton, and cooking oil all come directly from plants.

8

Viruses and Other Problems

Although we have talked about different classification systems in this book, we have focused on the five-kingdom system because we believe that it is the best system developed so far. Yet, even the five-kingdom system is not perfect. Why not? In this chapter we discuss two examples that do not fit well into any of the five kingdoms of life. Perhaps we need more kingdoms, or perhaps all we need is a clearer definition of what life is.

Viruses

Since their discovery, viruses (microscopic disease-causing agents) have been a problem for taxonomists. Even in the five-kingdom system, viruses continue to be difficult to classify. Most people know of viruses because their doctors often diagnose viruses as the culprit of their sicknesses. Colds, flus, herpes, and AIDS are all examples of diseases attributed to viruses (Figure 28).

Besides causing diseases in humans, viruses can afflict plants and fungi. They are a concern for farmers, since some, like tobacco mosaic virus, may sweep through and destroy whole fields of plants. Viruses even trouble bacteria. Figure 29 shows a virus infecting and killing a bacterial cell. Studies of bacteria-eating viruses, called bacterio-phages, were crucial to the development of the modern sciences of molecular biology and genetic engineering.

Although viruses can cause disease, most biologists do not con-sider them to be alive. Even if given food and energy, they do not grow or reproduce. Far smaller than cells, viruses do not do anything at all outside of cells; they act like chemicals—they have no need of water or food. Some look like hypodermic needles, others like space cap-sules; some can take the form of beautiful crystals (like snowflakes or diamonds), but all are merely pieces of the genetic material known as DNA or RNA wrapped up in a coating of protein. All viruses outside of living cells do nothing at all. Biologists who speak of viruses as alive are emphasizing their active role in certain diseases.

Viruses can act only inside a cell. Once inside, they take over the cell's production systems, alter its genetic information, and subvert a healthy cell into making more viruses—or into making tumor cells. This invasive and take-over activity that leads to new viruses shows up as a sickness or a new structure, or it may even go completely unnoticed.

Viruses are very important to the study of life on Earth and are more related to the cells that they enter (tobacco mosaic to tobacco, chicken pox to people) than they are to each other. Since they are deficient parts of cells, unable to do anything (including eat, breathe, or reproduce) until they enter cells, it seems unwise to give them their own kingdom. Nonetheless, some might argue that viruses are active enough inside cells to be considered alive and that therefore they qualify as a sixth kind of life.

Could Machines Be Alive?

Another possible candidate for separate kingdom status is even stranger: machines. Most people would say right away that machines are not alive. Humans make them, and they always require people to run and maintain them. But think about it: machines are very similar

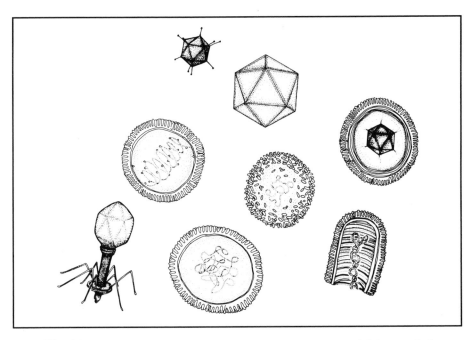

Fig. 28: Viruses come in many different sizes and shapes, but all have coiled nucleic acid inside a protein covering.

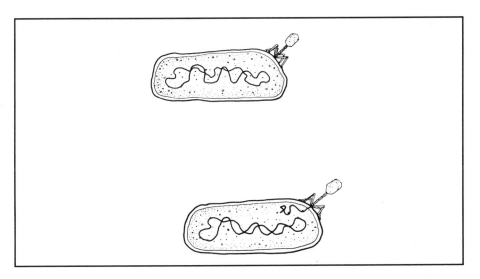

Fig. 29: The virus sticks to the surface of the bacterium (top) and injects its nucleic acid inside (bottom).

to viruses in this regard. Viruses need live cells to be active and lifelike, just as machines need people to manufacture them and to turn them on and off.

In the 19th century the English writer Samuel Butler (1835–1902) thought about life and machines from many different perspectives. He argued that machines, which of course were made by people, were now forming a new kingdom of life "stealing over the face of the earth." He even suggested that mechanical contraptions such as umbrellas and trains were parts of human beings. An umbrella, for example, is a detachable limb that protects people from rain; although made of whale bone (the old ones were) and cloth, it is a temporary part of the human body. A train, he reasoned, is like a huge moving limb, helping people move by means of a giant "foot" outside individual bodies.

In arguing that machines were evolving into a new kingdom, Butler pointed out that they are not completely different from past forms of life. You might say that a television set cannot be alive because it is made by workers in a factory, whereas a baby or tadpole, in contrast, comes directly from its mother's egg. If Butler were here today, though, he might remind us that many flowers cannot reproduce themselves directly either —they need the help of the insects that flit about gathering nectar, thereby transmitting male flower pollen to fertilize the female parts of the plant.

Butler would laugh if he visited us today. He would show us the television set airing a program on how to construct television sets, radio shows on making an inexpensive crystal radio, or a copying machine copying the blueprint of its own design. He would point out the "reproduction" of robots, if he toured the factories in which robots help make other robots. All are examples that could be viewed as machines reproducing themselves.

Could Butler be right? Take the telephone, the photocopier, and the fax machine—are they reproducing? Are they evolving? Do machines deserve to be classified as the newest kingdom of life?

Biology has been called "the science of the incredible." Thinking about the status of machines—whether they are alive or not, and if so, how—is a good way to begin studying taxonomy.

What Is Life?

Viruses and machines show us that even the five-kingdom taxonomy has problems. If viruses and machines are alive, then perhaps there are not just five but actually seven kingdoms of life. The Butlerian way of thinking leads us into deeper problems. Even for biologists, the question "What is life?" is not so easy to answer. For now, we accept the notion that, although it is difficult to define in words, we recognize life—bacterium, protoctist, fungus, animal, or plant—when we see it. Watery and flowing, moving and growing, responding to needs of energy and matter, life is changing constantly even as it stays the same.

9

Conclusion

Leeuwenhoek's discovery of a whole world of tiny organisms living beyond the focus of the human eye forced biologists to rethink what they knew about nature. Bacteria, first thought to be tiny plants or animals, are really ancestors. Bacteria did not evolve from plants or animals; rather plants, animals, protoctists, and fungi evolved from bacteria.

When different kinds of bacteria merged, they formed new cells with nuclei. These were the protoctists. From amebas to brown kelp bobbing in the middle of the sea, protoctists continue to evolve into many diverse forms. The rich variety of microbes and their communities provided the ancestral stock for plants, animals, and fungi. Like bacteria, which continued to exist separately even after some of them merged to become protoctists, protoctists also continued to exist after some of them became the oldest ancestors of plants, animals, and fungi.

Plants and animals are only the tip of the iceberg as far as life is concerned. They are newcomers on Earth's stage of life, and they owe their abilities—including photosynthesis, movement, behavior, and development—to the microbial planetmates that preceded them by at least two thousand million years.

Looking closely at the way classification systems change over time, we come to the realization that no taxonomy is permanent or perfect. Like the organisms they classify, taxonomies evolve. They change and grow with new knowledge, further insights, and new ways of thinking.

The five-kingdom system emphasizes the diversity of life on Earth. Biologists are beginning to understand the importance of different kinds of life coexisting in ways that keep living systems going. No plant or animal can live all alone. All plants and animals would starve or suffocate if there were no bacteria, fungi, or protoctists. Bacteria are the only kind of life that can survive without help from any other kingdom, but within the bacterial kingdom itself there are many types of cells, each capable of doing different things. In terms of the chemicals they use and where and how they live, bacteria—not animals or plants—are the most diverse organisms on Earth.

The five-kingdom system is important because it helps us see the differences and interdependencies among the many kinds of life that inhabit our living planet. Animals depend on plants. Plants (and some animals, such as certain ants) depend on fungi. We depend on plants for food, on fungi for penicillin, and so on.

All organisms depend on bacteria, which generally are noticed only when something fails; for instance, humans notice bacteria when they cause disease. When bacteria help us, as they usually do, we tend to take them for granted.

The health of all organisms depends upon diversity, on different sorts of organisms providing food and shelter for each other as they live next to or even inside of each other. Bacteria, fungi, and protoctists clean away the carcasses and refuse of animals and plants, restoring clean water, fertile soils, and breathable air. The five kinds of life work together like the fingers of a single hand—completely unconsciously.

Glossary

algae (singular: alga)—Protoctists that make their own food from carbon dioxide (CO_2) from the air and sunlight by photosynthesis. Algae include seaweeds and other water-dwelling organisms.

Animalia—The kingdom to which belong organisms that form from an embryo after a sperm fertilizes an egg.

ameba—A type of one-celled protoctist (protist) with a changeable shape that eats bacteria and other protists.

angiosperm—A plant that produces its seeds inside flowers.

bacteria (singular: bacterium)—Cells with no nucleus, either individual or forming groups, in which the DNA is not wrapped by proteins.

blastula—A ball of cells that develops from a fertile egg, making the kind of embryo from which all animals grow.

categorize—To classify or place something in a group.

cellulose—A hard compound in the walls of plant cells that makes plants rigid. Paper and wood contain cellulose.

chloroplasts—Green, light-using centers in algal and plant cells that capture energy. Scientists think that chloroplasts evolved from photosynthetic bacteria.

chromosomes—Structures in animal, plant, fungal, and protoctist cells in which the genes (DNA) are wrapped by proteins. Each cell has more than one chromosome.

cilium (plural: cilia)—A short undulipodium. A waving microscopic hair or whiplike structure that is made of tiny tubes (called microtubules) and facilitates the flow of water; found only in cells with nuclei.

classification—A grouping of things, such as a grouping of organisms by common features into taxonomic groups (such as kingdom, phylum, class, family, and species).

cyanobacteria (singular: cyanobacterium)—Photosynthetic microbes, once called blue-green algae. Cyanobacteria lack nuclei. These green-colored microbes are very common and are thought to be responsible for the build-up of oxygen in the atmosphere of the early Earth.

Euglena—A photosynthetic swimming cell with a nucleus. *Euglena* is difficult to classify in a two-kingdom system because it has traits of both plants and animals. The five-kingdom system recognizes this microbe as a protoctist.

eukaryote—An organism whose cells have nuclei. All protoctists, fungi, animals, and plants are eukaryotes.

fermentation—A process inside cells that converts sugars to alcohols or acids in the absence of oxygen gas.

five-kingdom system—The taxonomic system that puts all life forms into one of five kingdoms: Monera (bacteria), Protoctista (protoctists), Fungi (fungi), Plantae (plants), and Animalia (animals).

flagellum (plural: flagella)—The rotary fiber of swimming bacteria; similar to the undulipodium (cilium) of eukaryotes in function but far smaller.

Fungi (singular: fungus)—The Kingdom to which eukaryotic organisms that grow from spores and decompose organic matter belong. Molds, mushrooms, and yeasts.

gene—DNA molecules that are inherited by offspring from parents and that carry information for making proteins or other cell products.

genus (plural: genera)—A taxonomic category more inclusive than species but less inclusive than phyla. (Genus names are always written in italics.)

kingdom—The most inclusive taxonomic category: Plantae, Protoctista, etc. Some people divide life into two "superkingdoms" (bacteria and nonbacteria) or three (Archaea, Eubacteria and Eukarya).

meiosis—A type of division of the nucleus of an animal, plant, protoctist or fungal cell in which the number of chromosomes is reduced to one-half the original number. All Monera lack meiosis.

73

microbes/microorganisms—Beings too small to be seen with the unaided eye.

microtubule—A small, hollow, long tube, found in cells with nuclei, that is made of protein and used in cell division and cell movement.

mitochondria (singular: mitochondrion)—Energy-producing organelles of eukaryotic cells that use oxygen.

mitosis—The type of nuclear division in an animal, plant, protoctist, or fungal cell in which the number of chromosomes stays the same as the original number. Monera lack mitosis.

Monera—The kingdom to which all bacteria, including cyanobacteria belong.

morphology—The study of shape or form.

multicellular—Having many cells.

nucleus—The DNA-containing kernel or center of eukaryotic cells; DNA wrapped in membrane forms the nucleus.

organelle—A small body inside a cell.

photosynthesis—The process of using light, water, and carbon dioxide to produce carbohydrate (sugar), which is used as food.

phylum—A taxonomic group just below kingdom; it is much more inclusive than a genus.

placenta—The tissue with blood vessels that attaches the fetus to its mother's uterus; the afterbirth of mammals.

Plantae—The kingdom to which eukaryotic organisms, usually photosynthetic, that form from embryos inside the parent belong; plants include mosses and vascular plants.

plastid—A DNA-containing organelle of plant and algae cells. There are many kinds, with many colors (white, orange, etc.). Green plastids are called chloroplasts.

prokaryotes—Organisms made of bacterial cells (Members of the Kingdom Monera or Procaryotae).

Protoctista—The kingdom to which eukaryotic microbes and their larger relatives belong.

protist—A microscopic protoctist with only one or few cells.

protozoa—The old, two-kingdom system name for some microbes that were considered to be tiny animals.

respiration—The process of breathing or taking up oxygen that combines with food (organic compounds) to yield energy for cell processes.

species—The taxonomic group consisting of beings that can all mate and reproduce with each other. (Species names are always italicized.)

spirochetes—Long, thin bacteria that are rapid swimmers.

spores—Cells resistant to extreme environmental conditions (heat, dryness) that are distributed through the air or water and that can grow into bacteria, protoctists, fungi or plants when conditions become favorable.

symbiosis—The living together of two or more organisms of different species.

taxonomy—The science or art of identifying, giving names to, and classifying different types of organisms. A taxon is a group.

two-kingdom system—The old classification system in which all organisms were considered either plants or animals.

undulipodium—Cilium, sperm tail, or other type of "cell whip" with a complex structure (made of microtubules) found only in cells with nuclei. These "hairlike" organelles move cells through the water or move water over the surfaces of cells.

vascular plant—Cone-, flower-, or spore-bearing plants that have vascular tissue (vessels) to conduct water and food inside them.

virus—Genes covered with protein that do nothing until they enter the proper cell and reproduce using the cell's chemical processes.

Further Reading
and Related Materials

Books

Gest, H. *The World of Microbes.* Madison, Wis.: Science Tech Publishers, 1987.

Larousse Encyclopedia of Animal Life. New York: Paul Hamlyn, 1969.

McMenamin, M., and McMenamin, D. *The Emergence of Animals.* New York: Columbia University Press, 1989.

Margulis, L., and Sagan, D. *The Microcosmos Coloring Book.* Rochester, N.Y.: Ward's Natural Science Establishment, 1988.

Margulis, L., and Schwartz, K. *Five Kingdoms: An Illustrated Guide to the Phyla of Life on Earth.* New York: W. H. Freeman, 1988.

Morrison, P., and Morrison, P. *The Office of Charles and Ray Eames: Powers of Ten.* San Francisco: Scientific American Library, 1982.

Richardson, D. *The Vanishing Lichens.* Vancouver, Canada: David and Charles, 1975.

Sagan, D., and Margulis, L. *Garden of Microbial Delights: A Practical Guide to the Subvisible World.* Boston: Harcourt Brace Jovanovich, 1988.

Sagan, D., and Margulis, L. *Biospheres: From Earth to Space.* Hillside, N.J.: Enslow Publishers, 1989.

Sleigh, M. A. *Protozoa and Other Protists.* London: Edward Arnold, 1989.

Stanek, V. J. *The Pictorial Encyclopedia of the Animal Kingdom.* New York: Crown Publishers, 1970.

Periodicals

Kaveski, S., Margulis, L., and Mehos, D. "There's No Such Thing as a One-Celled Plant or Animal." *The Science Teacher.* December 1983, pp. 41–43.

Margulis, L. "How Many Kingdoms? Current Views of Biological Classification." *The American Biology Teacher.* December 1981, pp. 482–489.

Vidal, G. "The Oldest Eukaryotic Cells." *Scientific American.* February 1984, pp. 48–57.

Woese, C. R. "Archaebacteria." *Scientific American.* June 1981, pp. 98–122.

Slides, Videos, and Visual Aids*

Margulis, L., and Olendzenski, L. *Common Fungi: Teacher's Guide* (video). Rochester, N.Y.: Ward's Natural Science Establishment, 1991.

fungi video with specimens, catalog #873503; fungi video alone, catalog #1931200

Margulis, L. and Schwartz, K.V. *Animals* (40 35mm slides). Rochester, N.Y.: Ward's Natural Science Establishment, 1988.

Margulis, L., and Schwartz, K.V. *Fungi* (20 35mm slides). Rochester, N.Y.: Ward's Natural Science Establishment, 1987.

Margulis, L., and Schwartz, K.V. *Introduction to the Five Kingdoms* (20 35mm slides and teacher's guide). Rochester, N.Y.: Ward's Natural Science Establishment, 1987.

Margulis, L., and Schwartz, K.V. *Plants* (40 35mm slides). Rochester, N.Y.: Ward's Natural Science Establishment, 1988.

Margulis, L., and Schwartz, K.V. *Protoctista* (40 35mm slides). Rochester, N.Y.: Ward's Natural Science Establishment, 1988.

Teacher's Guide to the Five Kingdoms of Life. Ward's *Five Kinds of Life* poster to which students can add pictures and names of organisms, with classroom activity pamphlet. Rochester, N.Y.: Ward's Natural Science Establishment, 1992.

teacher's guide with poster, catalog #33W0024; poster alone, catalog #33W0025

*All are available from Ward's Natural Science Establishment, 5100 West Henrietta Road, P.O. Box 92912, Rochester, N.Y. 14692-9012; telephone: (800) 962-2660.

Index